# MY PLACE IN HISTORY

# My Journey on the
# UNDERGROUND RAILROAD

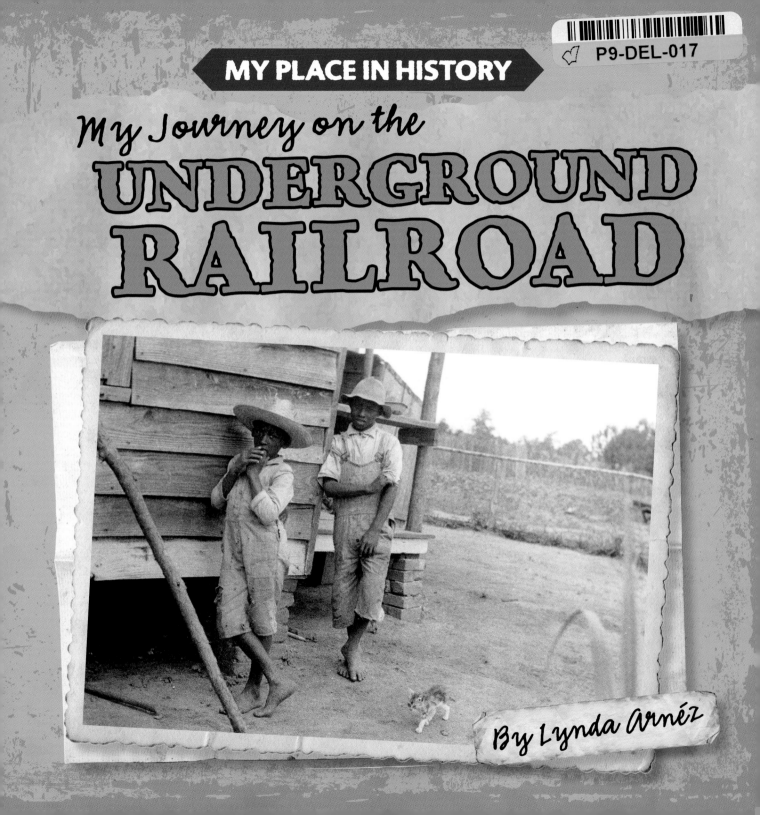

By Lynda Arnéz

Please visit our website, www.garethstevens.com. For a free color catalog of all our high-quality books, call toll free 1-800-542-2595 or fax 1-877-542-2596.

**Library of Congress Cataloging-in-Publication Data**

Arnéz, Lynda.
  My journey on the underground railroad / Lynda Arnéz.
      pages cm. — (My place in history)
  Includes index.
ISBN 978-1-4824-4010-2 (pbk.)
ISBN 978-1-4824-3996-0 (6 pack)
ISBN 978-1-4824-3997-7 (library binding)
1.  Underground Railroad—Juvenile literature. 2.  Fugitive slaves—United States—History—19th century—Juvenile literature. I. Title.
  E450.A77 2016
  973.7'115—dc23

                            2015031502

First Edition

Published in 2016 by
**Gareth Stevens Publishing**
111 East 14th Street, Suite 349
New York, NY 10003

Copyright © 2016 Gareth Stevens Publishing

Designer: Laura Bowen
Editor: Kristen Nelson

Photo credits: Cover, p. 1 (slave boys) ullstein bild/Wikimedia Commons; cover, pp. 1–24 (torn strip) barbaliss/Shutterstock.com; cover, pp. 1–24 (photo frame) Davor Ratkovic/Shutterstock.com; cover, pp. 1–24 (white paper) HABRDA/Shutterstock.com; cover, pp. 1–24 (parchment) M. Unal Ozmen/Shutterstock.com; cover, pp. 1–24 (textured edge) saki80/Shutterstock.com; cover (background) Natalia Sheinkin/Shutterstock.com; pp. 1–24 (paper background) Kostenko Maxim/Shutterstock.com; pp. 5, 15 (inset), 17 (main), 19 (both) Everett Historical/Shutterstock.com; p. 7 (main) Photo 12/Universal Images Group/Wikimedia Commons; p. 7 (inset) Mondadori/Getty Images; p. 9 (main) Universal Images Group/Getty Images; p. 9 (inset) Jupiterimages/Stockbyte/Getty Images; p. 11 Fotosearch/Archive Photos/Getty Images; p. 15 (main) Charles T. Webber/Wikimedia Commons; p. 17 (inset) DCPL Commons/Wikimedia Commons; p. 21 (Tubman) Cliffswallow-vaulting/Wikimedia Commons; p. 21 (Douglass, Still, Garrett) Scewing/Wikimedia Commons.

Printed in the United States of America

CPSIA compliance information: Batch #CW16GS: For further information contact Gareth Stevens, New York, New York at 1-800-542-2595.

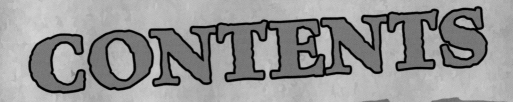

# CONTENTS

Words in the glossary appear in **bold** type the first time they are used in the text.

# Born a SLAVE

June 1, 1850

    If I could run away, I would. I'd take my mother and my little sister with me, too. We would leave Maryland, where we live on a small tobacco farm, and go north. It's not that our master is that mean. I've heard the older men talking in the fields about being hurt and not being given enough food when they worked for other masters.

    It doesn't matter how much he feeds us or how nice he is. We're still slaves—and I want to be free!

## Notes from History

Some slaves knew there were people and places that could help them escape, but they didn't have a name for it. Today, the many **routes** slaves traveled to freedom are called the Underground Railroad.

People who helped slaves to freedom often used railroad terms to **disguise** their activities. Those leading the slaves were "conductors," safe places to stop were called "stations," and the slaves were called "cargo" or "passengers."

# Learning to READ AND WRITE

June 20, 1850

Field slaves like me don't have to work on Sundays! One of the older slaves runs a little school for all of us in the afternoon. That's where I learned how to read and write. My mother works in the house, so she doesn't have Sundays off. I try to teach her what I've learned, though.

Today is also my eighth birthday. The pencil I'm writing with was a gift from my little sister. She's learning to write, too.

## Notes from History

In many southern states, it was illegal for slaves to learn to read and write. It wasn't outlawed in Maryland, but it wasn't supported either.

Slave boys often started working in the fields around age 6.

# A Day in THE FIELDS

July 15, 1850

I've been up since before dawn, working in and around the fields. It's very hot, and we only stop a few times a day for water. If I stop early, I might get **whipped** like my friend was when he tried to slip an apple to his brothers and sisters.

When I first started working in the fields, I pulled weeds and picked bugs off the tobacco plants. Now that I'm a little bigger, I also carry firewood and water for the other field workers.

## Notes from History

Children of slaves were born into slavery. Many would never know any other life.

Slaves often went hungry and had poor housing and few clothes. They had no rights. Their masters completely controlled their lives—and could be as **cruel** as they saw fit.

# Families LIVING APART

August 4, 1850

    My father hasn't lived with my mother, sister, and me in a long time. Mother has always said he's on a **plantation** in Virginia and that someday we'd see him again. That might happen soon! Mother spoke with a visitor's maid who knew him. She said my father has gone north to Canada!

    The maid told my mother of a place in Philadelphia where we could find help to meet him. But we'd have to get to Philadelphia ourselves first.

## Notes from History

Slave families didn't get to stay together very often. Masters bought and sold male slaves without caring whether they had children or a wife.

Families would go to great lengths to try to stay together—especially if it seemed like a son or father might be sold to a plantation further south where conditions were even worse for slaves.

# On the RUN!

August 14, 1850

In the darkest part of the night, my mother woke up my sister and me. She told us to keep quiet and move fast. She'd already packed up everything we own! I'm glad she included my little pencil. We started walking—and kept going until we were off the farm!

The sun just started to rise. We're hiding together in a **shack** in the woods. I don't know how far we've come or how far we need to go. I'm so scared we'll be caught.

## Notes from History

Slaves traveling the Underground Railroad often started their journey alone. Knowledge of conductors or safe houses was sometimes carried by word of mouth, but many slaves escaped without knowing help was available.

# THE UNDERGROUND RAILROAD

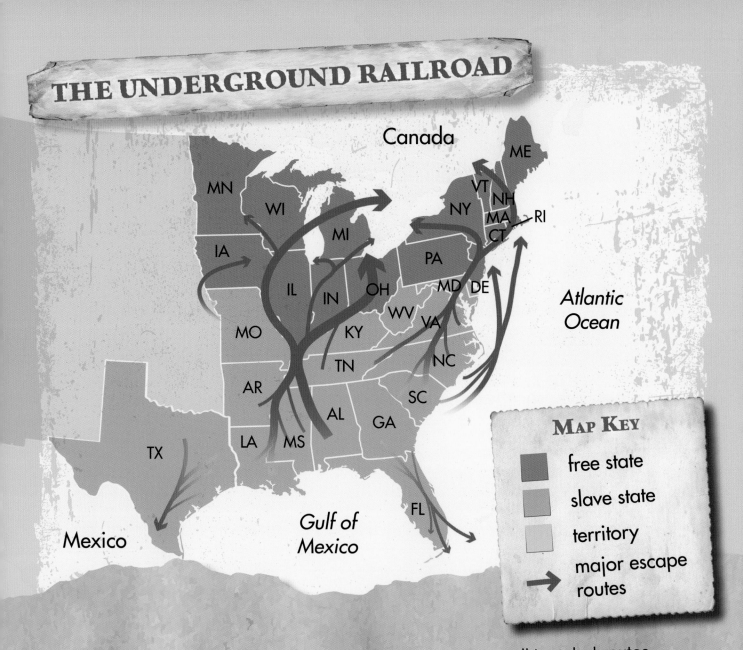

The Underground Railroad was made up of some well-traveled routes north, but a slave's journey depended on what state they came from and their **destination**. As this map shows, some slaves fled south, too!

# safe HOUSE

September 1850

    I lost track of how many nights we walked. About a week ago, we met up with another group of escaped slaves, including the maid who had given my mother news about my father! My mother said the only thing we could do was trust them.

    I'm glad we did! We're hiding in the home of a free black man named William Still. He says we're in Philadelphia, Pennsylvania, and that we must be **patient** before the next part of our journey.

## Notes from History

Conductors on the Underground Railroad included free blacks like Still, as well as escaped slaves and even some whites.

William Still kept notes about the **fugitives** he helped. He destroyed these to **protect** the escaped slaves, but later wrote a book about his work on the Underground Railroad. Still helped almost 800 slaves escape.

WILLIAM STILL

# The Law CHANGES

October 1850

Mr. Still is preparing us to keep heading north. He said that slaves used to be able to just come to a northern state where slavery was illegal and be free. There's a new law that says any escaped slaves, if found, must be returned to their master. Anyone who helps us is breaking the law, too!

Mr. Still and his friends tell us we just need to be even more careful. They're abolitionists, which means they believe all slavery should be outlawed.

## Notes from History

Slave owners sometimes offered **rewards** to people who brought their slaves back to them.

**$100 REWARD.**

Ranaway from the subscriber's farm, near Washington, on the 11th of October, negro woman SOPHIA GORDON, about 24 years of age, rather small in size, of copper color, is tolerably good looking, has a low and soft manner of speech. She is believed to be among associates formed in Washington where she has been often hired.

I will give the above reward, no matter where taken and secured in jail so that I get her again.
GEORGE W. YOUNG.

November 16th, 1858.

H. Polkinhorn's Steam Job Printing Office, D street, bet 4th & 7th sts., Washington, D C

Despite the law, called the Fugitive Slave Act of 1850, the Underground Railroad continued to work hard leading up to the **American Civil War**.

# Walk by NIGHT

October 1850

   We left Philadelphia with another family from North Carolina. At first, the eight of us hid in the back of a wagon. Then, we stayed for a few days at another safe house. Our guide came one night, and we've been walking ever since.

   Just like when we were trying to get to Philadelphia, we've been traveling at night and hiding during the day. My little sister is tired after hours of walking, so Mother and I take turns carrying her on our backs.

## Notes from History

Some slaves reached freedom by hiding in boxes or in the bottoms of boats. Others wore disguises and simply crossed into a northern state or Canada!

Those on the Underground Railroad had to travel through fields and forests and even cross frozen rivers to freedom. Historians believe between 40,000 and 100,000 slaves were aided by the Underground Railroad before the Civil War.

# Free AT LAST

November 1850

It's starting to get very cold, especially at night. I've been afraid we wouldn't reach Canada before the first heavy snowfall. But here we are! Last night, our guide brought us to our last safe house. A new guide told us it was the perfect night to cross the border.

We still have to meet up with my father, but Mother has already heard that he passed through here. Once we find him, our family can finally be together—and free!

## Notes from History

The Underground Railroad wasn't always successful. Family members were often left behind, and some slaves were caught and punished. Reaching Canada truly was an accomplishment.

# Famous Underground Railroad Conductors

**Harriet Tubman**
escaped slave; guided hundreds of slaves to freedom herself

**Frederick Douglass**
borrowed papers saying he was free to escape slavery; gave speeches against slavery; ran one of the final stations before the Canadian border

**William Still**
free black man; housed many fugitives in Philadelphia and helped them get to Canada

**Thomas Garrett**
white man from Delaware; helped fugitives get to Pennsylvania; worked with Harriet Tubman

**John Parker**
born a slave; led slaves from Kentucky to his home in Ohio

# GLOSSARY

**American Civil War:** a war fought from 1861 to 1865 in the United States between the Union (the Northern states) and the Confederacy (the Southern states)

**cruel:** causing others hurt without feeling sorry about it

**destination:** the place to which somebody or something is going

**disguise:** to hide. Also, a way of dressing meant to hide who one is.

**fugitive:** a slave who was trying to escape to freedom

**patient:** calm and able to wait a long time

**plantation:** a large farm

**protect:** to keep safe

**reward:** money paid for doing something

**route:** a course that people travel

**shack:** a small, roughly built shelter

**whip:** to strike with a rod, rope, or strip of leather attached to a handle

# For more INFORMATION

## Books

Coleman, Wim. *Follow the Drinking Gourd: Come Along the Underground Railroad.* South Egremont, MA: Red Chair Press, 2015.

Conkling, Winifred. *Passenger on the Pearl: The True Story of Emily Edmonson's Flight from Slavery.* Chapel Hill, NC: Algonquin Young Readers, 2015.

Hyde, Natalie. *The Underground Railroad.* New York, NY: Crabtree Publishing Company, 2015.

## Websites

**Pathways to Freedom: Maryland & the Underground Railroad**
*pathways.thinkport.org/about/about1.cfm*
Learn much more about the Underground Railroad, and complete some related activities.

**The Underground Railroad**
*education.nationalgeographic.com/underground-railroad-interactive/#*
Use this interactive website to understand what slaves went through on the Underground Railroad.

# INDEX